#6413

D1717021

This book given
by
Alice Fabro Edwards
in memory of her husband
Bill Edwards
2002

DISCARD

DISCARD

The United States

Tennessee

Paul Joseph
ABDO & Daughters

SOUTHWEST
MEDIA CENTER

visit us at
www.abdopub.com

Published by Abdo & Daughters, 4940 Viking Drive, Suite 622, Edina, Minnesota 55435.
Copyright © 1998 by Abdo Consulting Group, Inc., Pentagon Tower, P.O. Box 36036,
Minneapolis, Minnesota 55435 USA. International copyrights reserved in all countries.
No part of this book may be reproduced in any form without written permission from the
publisher.

Printed in the United States.

Cover and Interior Photo credits: Peter Arnold, Inc., SuperStock, Archive

Edited by Lori Kinstad Pupeza
Contributing editor Brooke Henderson
Special thanks to our Checkerboard Kids—Teddy Borth, John Hansen, Aisha Baker

State population statistics taken from the 2000 census, city population statistics taken
from the 1990 census; U.S. Census Bureau.

Library of Congress Cataloging-in-Publication Data

Joseph, Paul, 1970-
        Tennessee / Paul Joseph.
        p.   cm. -- (The United States)
        Includes index.
        Summary: Surveys the history, geography, people, cities, and other aspects of
        the state known for its natural beauty.
        ISBN 1-56239-875-X
        1. Tennessee--Juvenile literature. [1. Tennessee.] I. title. II. Series: United
        States (Series).
        F436.3.J67 1998
        976.8--dc21   97-20636
                                                                            CIP
                                                                            AC

Contents

Welcome to Tennessee

The state of Tennessee sits on a narrow strip of land in the south-central section of the United States. It is **bordered** by eight other states. No other state is bordered by more states than that.

Tennessee is sometimes thought of as three different states because of the differences in land and customs. The Great Smoky Mountains tower over Tennessee's thickly wooded land. Rolling farmland, foothills, and pastures cover the middle of Tennessee. And western Tennessee is known for its cotton **industry**.

Tennessee got its name from the **Native American** word *Tanasi*. It was the name of a Cherokee village on the Little Tennessee River. Its nickname, the Volunteer State, came from the large number of people from Tennessee who volunteered to fight in the War of 1812. More people volunteered from Tennessee than any other state.

Nashville and Memphis are famous for country music. Tennessee has also been home to three presidents of the United States: Andrew Jackson, James K. Polk, and Andrew Johnson. The man known as the King of Rock-n-Roll, Elvis Presley, lived most of his life in Tennessee.

The Great Smoky Mountains in Tennessee.

Fast Facts

TENNESSEE

Capital
Nashville (487,969 people)
Area
42,144 square miles
(109,152 sq km)
Population
5,689,283 people
Rank: 16th
Statehood
June 1, 1796
(16th state admitted)
Principal rivers
Mississippi River
Tennessee River
Highest point
Clingmans Dome;
6,643 feet (2,025 m)
Largest city
Memphis (610,337 people)
Motto
Agriculture and commerce
Song
"The Tennessee Waltz" and four
others
Famous People
Davy Crokett, Dolly Parton,
Albert Gore, Andrew Johnson,
Andrew Jackson

*S*tate Flag

*I*ris

*M*ockingbird

*T*ulip Poplar

About Tennessee

The Volunteer State

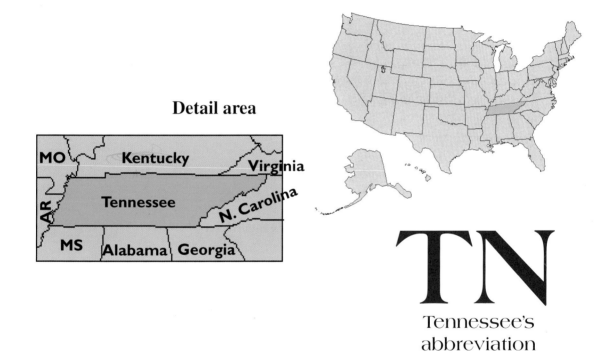

Detail area

MO
Kentucky
Virginia
AR
Tennessee
N. Carolina
MS
Alabama
Georgia

TN
Tennessee's abbreviation

Borders: west (Arkansas, Missouri), north (Kentucky, Virginia), east (North Carolina), south (Mississippi, Alabama, Georgia)

Nature's Treasures

Tennessee has many wonderful treasures in its state. There are scenic mountains, many lakes and rivers, National Parks, excellent farmland, and valuable **minerals** under the ground.

The best known treasure in Tennessee is the Great Smoky Mountains. These beautiful mountains are in the eastern part of the state. The mountains are named for the blue-gray haze that covers their peaks. **Tourists** visit this land for the scenery.

The farmland in Tennessee is another treasure. There are about 91,000 farms in the state. The major crops grown on the land are corn, cotton, wheat, soybeans, and tobacco.

Underground the state has treasures in minerals. The valuable minerals found underground include stone, coal, and zinc.

The waters of Tennessee are also treasures. Different fish like buffalofish, catfish, and bullheads swim in Tennessee's lakes and rivers.

Waterfalls in the Great Smoky Mountains National Park.

Beginnings

The first known people to live in Tennessee were **Native Americans.** The largest group were the Cherokee, who lived in the eastern part of the state. In the south were the Shawnee and in the west were the Chickasaw.

By 1800, Europeans had taken over the land and only the Cherokee remained in Tennessee. However, during the 1830s, the Cherokee were forced out too. They moved to the Indian Territory, which is now the state of Oklahoma.

It is believed that the first European to enter Tennessee was Hernando de Soto in 1540. More than 100 years later, in 1682, French **explorer** Robert La Salle claimed the land for France. In 1763, France gave the land to England.

New settlers began coming to the state. Most of these settlers were from eastern states and were of English, Irish, French, and German descent. The land became part of the United States.

In 1861, Tennessee left the **Union** and joined the **Confederacy** in the **Civil War**. The Civil War was fought because the South wanted to keep slavery legal.

There were many battles between the North and the South. The North finally won the Civil War and Tennessee freed its slaves in 1865. Tennessee was the first southern state readmitted to the Union after the war, on July 24, 1866.

The Battle of Corinth, the Civil War.

B.C. to 1760

Early Land and Explorers

During the Ice Age, thousands of years ago, Tennessee was covered by huge glaciers of ice. Many years later the ice began to melt and the land of Tennessee began to form.

The first known people to live in Tennessee were **Native Americans.** They were the Cherokee, Shawnee, and Chickasaw.

1540: Hernando de Soto camps near the present site of Memphis.

1682: Robert La Salle claims Tennessee for France.

1760: Daniel Boone explores eastern Tennessee.

12

Tennessee

B.C. to 1760

1796 to 1866

Statehood and Beyond

1796: Tennessee becomes the 16th state on June 1.

1861: Tennessee leaves the **Union** and joins the **Confederacy**.

1861-5: Many **Civil War** battles are fought in the state. Only Virginia had more battles.

1866: After the North defeats the South in the Civil War, Tennessee is the first Confederate state to be readmitted into the Union.

Tennessee

1796 to 1866

1967 to Now

Present Day Tennessee

 1967: The Nickajack Dam is completed.

 1975: Hundreds are evacuated during the worst flood in Tennessee history.

 1988: A **drought** disaster is declared. It is the worst drought since the 1930s.

 1992: Tennessee native Albert Gore is elected vice president of the United States.

16

Tennessee

1967 to Now

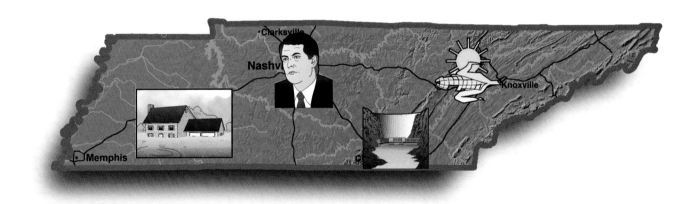

Tennessee's People

There are close to five million people living in the state of Tennessee. It is the 17th most populated state in the country.

There are many well-known people who have made Tennessee home. Andrew Jackson was the seventh president of the United States. He lived near Nashville. He was a Tennessee lawyer, then a congressman, judge, and a general in the War of 1812. In 1828, he was elected president.

Two other people who lived for a while in Tennessee were also presidents. James K. Polk was the 11th president of the United States. Before becoming president he was the governor of Tennessee. Andrew Johnson of Greeneville was the vice president under Abraham Lincoln. When Lincoln was **assassinated** in 1865, Johnson became the 17th president.

The vice president of the United States, Albert Gore, is from Tennessee. Before becoming vice president in 1992, he was a United States Senator from Tennessee.

Elvis Presley, who is known as the King of Rock-n-Roll lived in Memphis. His home, called Graceland, is one of the biggest **tourist** attractions in the world.

Other famous people from Tennessee are entertainer Dolly Parton, football player Lynn Swann, and **civil rights** leader Mary Church Terrell.

Vice President Al Gore

Dolly Parton

Elvis Presley

Splendid Cities

Tennessee has many splendid cities in its state. Some are very large cities while others are small **rural** towns. The state also has many famous cities that are known throughout the world.

Tennessee has four cities with **populations** of more than 100,000. Memphis, the largest city with just over 600,000 people, is a busy port center on the Mississippi River. It is an important cotton and lumber market.

The capital, Nashville, is the second largest city. It is located in the center of the state on the Cumberland River. Nashville is also very famous for the Grand Ole Opry. The Opry has been doing a live radio show since 1925.

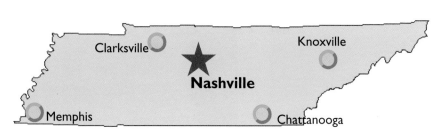

Andrew Jackson's home is also located in Nashville.

Knoxville, the third largest city, is located in the heart of the Tennessee Valley. Chattanooga, the next largest city, lies on the Tennessee River, in the southeast.

Other splendid cities include Oak Ridge, Jackson, Bristol, Clarksville, Johnson City, Murfreesboro, Kingsport, and Germantown to name a few.

Nashville is Tennessee's second largest city.

Tennessee's Land

Tennessee has some of the most beautiful and diverse land in the country. A person can find rivers, mountains, lakes, forests, rich farmland, and valleys. The narrow state is divided into seven different regions.

The Blue Ridge is a rugged, narrow, mountainous area in the very eastern part of the state. The Great Smoky Mountains are located in this region. Within them is Clingmans Dome. This is the highest point in the state at 6,643 feet (2,025 m).

The Valley and Ridge region is just west of the Blue Ridge. Jagged land covers this area. The Cumberland Plateau is just west of the Valley and Ridge region. It has steep hills. The Highland Rim is a region

near the center of the state. It is the largest region in the state and covers many small ravines and streams.

The Nashville Basin is a circle in the middle of the state. It has the state's finest farmland.

The Gulf Coastal Plain is the second largest region in the state. It reaches from the lower Tennessee River to the bluffs overlooking the Mississippi River.

The Mississippi Floodplain is a small region located on the western edge of the state. The area is dotted with small lakes and marshes. In the extreme south is the lowest point in the state at 182 feet (55 m) above sea level.

Bald Cypress Reelfoot National Wildlife Refuge in Tennessee.

Tennessee at Play

Tennessee is a great place to play. There are so many different things to do and see in the state.

Many people visit the state each year. **Tourism** is a very big **industry** in the state. Two of the biggest things to see are the Great Smoky Mountains National Park and Cumberland Gap National Historical Park.

Some **tourists** visit the wonderful state parks in Tennessee. Some of the state parks include Chickasaw, Cove Lake, David Crockett, and Fall Creek Falls.

The many rivers and lakes in the state offer the best in water sports. People swim, ski, fish, boat, and canoe in the waters of Tennessee.

The American Museum of Science and Energy at Oak Ridge draws many tourists. The state fair each September in Nashville draws thousands of people for fun and games.

The theme park Opryland USA and the Country Music Hall of Fame and Museum also in Nashville are popular attractions. However, **tourists** seem to visit Graceland the most.

Geer Springs National Scenic River is a popular attraction in Tennessee.

SOUTHWEST SCIENCE MEDIA CENTER

Tennessee at Work

The people of Tennessee must work to make money. Many people work in or around large cities, while others work in **rural** communities.

The number one **industry** in the state is **manufacturing**. Many people in the state work in this industry. Some of the manufacturing businesses include machinery, chemicals, food products, and electronic equipment.

Many people in the state are farmers. The state has about 91,000 farms. Some of the crops that farmers grow are soybeans, tobacco, corn, cotton, and wheat.

Some people in the state work as miners. Coal was once the most valuable **mineral** mined but now is second to crushed stone.

There are many different things to do and see in the great state of Tennessee. Because of its natural beauty, people, land, mountains, and **tourist** attractions, Tennessee is a great place to visit, live, work, and play.

Catfish farming on the Mississippi river.

Fun Facts

•When Tennessee became a state in 1796, Knoxville was the capital. From 1818 to 1826, Murfreesboro was the capital. In 1843, the capital was moved to Nashville where it still is today.

•In 1811 and 1812, Tennessee suffered many major earthquakes. Because of these earthquakes the Reelfoot Lake was created.

•Tennessee has been the home of three presidents of the United States—Andrew Jackson, James K. Polk, and Andrew Johnson.

•The first American guide dog for the blind lived in Nashville, Tennessee. The German shepherd was trained in 1928. Its name was Buddy.

The Tennessee State Capitol in Nashville.

Glossary

Assassinated: the murder of a very important person.

Border: neighboring states, countries, or waters.

Civil Rights: The rights of a citizen. These rights are written down in the Constitution.

Civil War: a war between groups within the same country.

Confederacy: a group that bands together for a common belief. In this case it is the 11 southern states that left the Union between 1860 and 1861.

Drought: a long time without getting any rain.

Explorers: people that are one of the first to discover and look over land.

Industry: many different types of businesses.

Manufacture: to make things by machine in a factory.

Minerals: things found in the earth, such as rock, diamonds, or coal.

Native Americans: the first people who were born in and occupied North America.

Population: the number of people living in a certain place.

Rural: outside of the city.

Tourism: a business that serves people who are traveling for pleasure, and visiting places of interest.

Tourists: people who travel for pleasure.

Union: the states that remained loyal to America during the Civil War were called the Union. The Union was against slavery.